I ♥ POO!

An Odd Squad book for POO LOVERS everywhere!
by Allan Plenderleith

ℜ
RAVETTE PUBLISHING

First Published by
Ravette Publishing Limited 2005
Unit 3, Tristar Centre, Star Road, Partridge Green,
West Sussex RH13 8RA

Printed and bound in Malta

ISBN: 1 84161 240 5

From his angle, Jeff was mistakenly convinced his clever dog could do a handstand.

Judging by all the 'chocolate kisses' on the floor
the dog's bum was in need of a wash again.

Lily accidentally steps in a giant
crack in the pavement.

Billy finally discovers where his
good crayons had gone.

If you're going to poo outside, remember to pull
your g-string down first.

Unable to flush her huge poo down her host's toilet, Maude simply hides it in her handbag.

Annoyingly, the cat was always too forceful
when covering up its business.

If you plan to frighten an old person by banging a crisp bag, it's best to do it from the front.

Unfortunately, when Maude had said she wanted Jeff to do something kinky in bed, he had misheard.

Never blow off in the doggy position.

Dug had eaten one too many curly wurlies.

At the barber's, Jeff asked for a 'Number Two'.

Mid-poo, Billy's toilet paper ran out.

The Odd Squad Guide to

'THE FIREBALL'

HOT AND PAINFUL.
MAY SINGE
BOTTOM HAIRS.

'THE CHOP OFF'

POO IS STOPPED
HALF-WAY DUE TO
PHONE RINGING ETC.

'THE STICKY'

STICKS TO HAIRS.
REQUIRES HOURS OF
WIPING.

'THE VEGGIE'

LOOKS AND SMELLS
EXACTLY LIKE A
VEGGIE BURGER.

'THE FIREHOSE'

MAINLY WATER-BASED.
CREATES HUGE MESS.

'THE CROQUETTES'

CRISPY ON THE OUTSIDE
WITH A LIGHT, PUFFY
CENTRE.

'THE SLIPPY'

SLIPS OUT IN ONE, SWIFT MOVEMENT. REQUIRES NO WIPING.

"THE STINKER'

REEKS SO BAD YOU DON'T EVEN RECOGNISE THE SMELL.

'THE BLIP'

SMALL BUT CAUSES BIG SPLASH.

'THE NEVERENDING STORY'

AN AMAZING ACHIEVEMENT. MAY NEED TO STAND TO ACCOMPLISH FULL LENGTH.

'THE SWEETCORN'
MOST COLOURFUL AND ATTRACTIVE.

'THE JAGGY'
CAUSED BY EATING TOO MANY CRISPS. MAY RESULT IN SURGERY.

'THE POPPETS'
COME OUT LIKE MACHINE GUN BULLETS.

'THE STEAMY HEAPY'
WILL NEVER FLUSH.

THE CHINESE MEAL POO

NICE AT THE TIME BUT ULTIMATELY UNSATISFYING. YOU'LL FEEL LIKE ANOTHER ONE IN HALF AN HOUR.

THE McBURGER POO

DRY, OVERCOOKED, AND EACH POO IS IDENTICAL . WARNING: MAY CONTAIN TEENAGE STAFF'S BOGIES!

THE INDIAN MEAL POO

A REAL ARSE BURNER. SITTING DOWN
WILL BE IMPOSSIBLE FOR WEEKS.
KEEP FIRE EXTINGUISHER HANDY.

THE FISH + CHIPS POO

A SUCCULENT POO WITH A CRISPY OUTER COATING. FOLLOWED BY A SIDE PORTION OF MUSHY PEE POO!

Once again, the dog had swallowed the
icing bag nozzle.

Never blow off in a g-string.

Billy impressed his friends with
his very own 'poo bear'.

Why it's always a good idea to sit at
the front on a roller coaster.

Maude was about to say how nice the new jacuzzi was, when she noticed something.

Jeff discovers one advantage to a poo
that won't break off.

Billy wondered if he'd followed through
on that last fart.

If her date's shadow was anything to go by,
this was going to be one hell of a night!

Jeff walked into the garden to find it
full of toad stools.

Jeff enters another
'wipe it or leave it' dilemma.

1. The Disappearing Poo!

It's always a big one, but when you look round it's gone!! No-one can explain this frustrating mystery.

Where is it?! I'm **SURE** I did one!

2. Splashback!

Occurs with small poos.
They create a huge splash
covering you in toilet water.
Most unpleasant.

AAA!

3. The Unflushable Poo!

Does not budge after repeated flushings.

Options:

1. Chop it with a knife
2. Fish it out with tongs and dispose safely.

OR   3. Live with it.

4. The Reluctant Poo!

The poo that comes out half way and stops. Only option is to slice in half with sphincter.

Come on! What's the hold up!?

5. The Neverending Wipe!

You keep on wiping but
you NEVER get clean!
You may be there for days.
(World Record stands at 7 years)

Over the years, Jeff had learned to read
the dog's mind.

Once again, Billy's worm was constipated.

A wet fart is bad at any time, but worse
when you're wearing shorts.

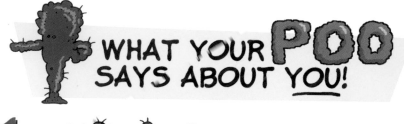

WHAT YOUR POO SAYS ABOUT YOU!

1.

YOU'RE A VERY GENEROUS, GIVING PERSON.
ALTHOUGH YOU GIVE SO MUCH IT LEAVES
YOU FEELING EMPTY INSIDE.

2.

A MESSY AND
IMPULSIVE PERSON.
WHEN YOU DECIDE TO
DO SOMETHING YOU
DROP EVERYTHING
AND GO!

3.

A SADO-MASOCHIST! YOU ENJOY PAIN BUT YOU DO HAVE A TENDER SIDE. (IE. YOUR TENDER BACKSIDE!)

4.

A REAL SNAKE IN THE GRASS! YOU'RE A SLIPPERY CUSTOMER WHO LIKES TO LEAVE NASTY SURPRISES IN LONG GRASS!

5.  YOU NEVER FINISH ANYTHING, ALWAYS CUTTING OFF JOBS HALF WAY THROUGH!

6.

YOU'RE A VERY COLOURFUL PERSON WITH A CORNY SENSE OF HUMOUR!

7.  STINGY GIT.

YOU'RE A VERY NEAT PERSON WHO NEVER LEAVES ANY MESS. BUT YOU'RE ALSO SLIGHTLY BORING.

COLD AND EVIL WITH A HEART OF STONE. YOU LIKE TO HURT SMALL ANIMALS.

Unfortunately, in an effort to smell his own fart, Jeff had bent back too far.

Jeff plays that popular party game
'Guess the REAL walnut whip!'

Jeff had a feeling the hamster had
trapped wind again.

Unfortunately, during his sensual massage,
Jeff relaxed a little too much.

Jeff's anal exam was not going well.

Patsy thought there was nothing more
embarrassing than accidentally tucking loo roll
into your knickers - she was wrong...

Jeff thought of the perfect burglar-proof disguise for his iPod.

Suddenly, Patsy's secret stash of chocolate
makes an unexpected appearance.

Maude was suprised to wake up on her birthday to a big, sparkling ring.

Jeff couldn't understand why Maude refused to have a look at his chocolate starfish.

HOW YOUR POOS CHANGE AS YOU GET OLDER!

BABY POO

LIKE NUCLEAR CABBAGE ONLY MORE DEADLY. DO NOT LET IT COME IN CONTACT WITH YOUR SKIN.

TEENAGE POO

JUST A BIG BALL OF LARD, MADE FROM A DIET OF BURGERS, PIZZAS & CHOCOLATE. HIGHLY INFECTIOUS.

TWENTYSOMETHING POO

POO IS GREEN DUE TO SUDDEN HEALTH KICK. BUT MORE VEG IN DIET MEANS SMELLIER POOS.

THIRTYSOMETHING POO

INCREASE IN DINNER PARTIES MEANS POOS BECOME DARKER AND RICHER IN QUALITY. THE BOUQUET IS ALMOST PLEASANT.

FORTYSOMETHING POO

MIDDLE AGE SPREAD SETS IN. POOS BECOME HUGE SWOLLEN MONSTROSITIES, JUST LIKE THEIR BIG ARSES.

OLD AGED POO (O.A.P.)

POOS ARE GREY, WRINKLY, DRIED UP AND SMELL LIKE ROTTING FLESH. JUST LIKE AN OLD PERSON REALLY!

Unfortunately, the strain of pushing was
too much for Strong Man Stu.

Lily had a feeling Billy had been watching
a scary movie in his bedroom again.

Unfortunately, moments too late, Jeff discovered the bird poo in his pint.

The 'Who can do the Biggest Fart Game' goes awry when Maude loses control for a secor

Fun uses for a TURTLE HEAD!

1. Great for pointing directions!

2. Handy as a children's coat hanger!

3. A springboard for dive-loving hamsters!

4. Great for performing amazing levitation tricks!

Other ODD SQUAD books available ...

		ISBN	Price
The Odd Squad's Big Poo Handbook	(hardcover)	1 84161 168 9	£7.99
The Odd Squad's Sexy Sex Manual	(hardcover)	1 84161 220 0	£7.99
The Odd Squad Butt Naked		1 84161 190 5	£3.99
The Odd Squad Gross Out!		1 84161 219 7	£3.99
The Odd Squad's Saggy Bits		1 84161 218 9	£3.99
The REAL Kama Sutra		1 84161 103 4	£3.99
The Odd Squad Volume One		1 85304 936 0	£3.99
I Love Beer!	(hardcover)	1 84161 238 3	£4.99
I Love Sex!	(hardcover)	1 84161 241 3	£4.99
I Love Wine!	(hardcover)	1 84161 239 1	£4.99
The Odd Squad's Little Book of Booze		1 84161 138 7	£2.50
The Odd Squad's Little Book of Men		1 84161 093 3	£2.50
The Odd Squad's Little Book of Oldies		1 84161 139 5	£2.50
The Odd Squad's Little Book of Poo		1 84161 096 8	£2.50
The Odd Squad's Little Book of Pumping		1 84161 140 9	£2.50
The Odd Squad's Little Book of Sex		1 84161 095 X	£2.50
The Odd Squad's Little Book of Women		1 84161 094 1	£2.50
The Odd Squad's Little Book of X-Rated Cartoons		1 84161 141 7	£2.50

HOW TO ORDER: Please send a cheque/postal order in £ sterling, made payable to 'Ravette Publishing' for the cover price of the books and allow the following for post & packing ...

UK & BFPO	60p for the first book & 30p per book thereafter
Europe & Eire	£1.00 for the first book & 50p per book thereafter
Rest of the world	£1.80 for the first book & 80p per book thereafter

VETTE PUBLISHING
3, Tristar Centre, Star Road, Partridge Green, West Sussex RH13 8RA

nd availability are subject to change without prior notice.